First of the Last Chances

SOPHIE HANNAH was born in Manchester in 1971. A former Fellow Commoner in Creative Arts at Trinity College, Cambridge and Fellow of Wolfson College, Oxford, she now lives in Bingley, West Yorkshire and teaches in the Writing School at Manchester Metropolitan University. Sophie Hannah is the author of three best-selling collections of poetry, as well as three novels and several books for children.

Also by Sophie Hannah

Fiction
Gripless
Cordial and Corrosive
The Superpower of Love

Poetry
The Hero and the Girl Next Door
Hotels Like Houses
Leaving and Leaving You
The Box Room

Translation
The Book about Moomin, Mymble and Little My

SOPHIE HANNAH

First of the Last Chances

CARCANET

First published in Great Britain in 2003 by
Carcanet Press Limited
4th Floor, Conavon Court
12–16 Blackfriars Street
Manchester M3 5BQ

A CIP catalogue record for this book
is available from the British Library

ISBN 1 85754 626 1

The publisher acknowledges financial assistance
from the Arts Council of England

Set in Monotype Garamond by XL Publishing Services, Tiverton
Printed and bound in England by SRP Ltd, Exeter

For Phoebe with love

Acknowledgements

Some of these poems have previously appeared in the following publications: *The Times Literary Supplement, Critical Quarterly, The New Delta Review, The Hudson Review, Mslexia, PN Review, Poetry Review, The Gift: New Writing for the NHS* (Stride), *Earth Has Not Anything to Shew More Fair* (Shakespeare's Globe and the Wordsworth Trust), *Last Words: New Poetry for the New Century* (Picador).

'Brief Encounter' was commissioned by First NorthWestern Trains, 'Where to Look' was commissioned by Acoustiguide for the reopening of Manchester City Art Gallery, and 'Seasonal Dilemma' was commissioned by the British Council for their 2001 Christmas card.

The eight poems of 'A Woman's Life and Loves' were commissioned by Ann Martin-Davis for a music touring project called 'Cycles'. 'Cycles' was sponsored by ClearBlue and produced with funds from the RVW Trust, the Britten–Pears Foundation, the Performing Right Society Foundation for New Music, Southern and South East Arts, and the Arts Council of England.

Contents

Long for This World	9
You Won't Find a Bath in Leeds	10
Out of This World	12
Wells-Next-the-Sea	13
Six of One	14
Seasonal Dilemma	15
Second-hand Advice for a Friend	16
Dark Mechanic Mills	17
Martins Heron Heart	18
Tide to Land	19
The Shadow Tree	20
He is Now a Country Member	21
Silk Librarian	22
God's Eleventh Rule	23
Where to Look	25
Brief Encounter	26
The Cycle	27
Black River	28
The Cancellation	29
The Guest Speaker	31
Everyone in the Changing Room	32
Your Funeral	33
Away-day	35
Mother-to-be	36
Now and Then	37
Healing Powers	38
Homeopathy	39
Your Turn Next	41
To a Certain Person	42
0208	43
Leave	45
Ante-Natal	46
On Westminster Bridge	47
Ballade of the Rift	48
Wedding Poem	49
Royal Wedding Poem	50
GODISNOWHERE (Now Read Again)	51
Metaphysical Villanelle	52
Squirrel's the Word	53
First of the Last Chances	54

A Woman's Life and Loves

View	57
Equals	58
Postcard	59
Match	60
Bridesmaid	61
Test	62
Charge	63
Favourite	64

Long for This World

I settle for less than snow,
try to go gracefully as seasons go

which will regain their ground –
ditch, hill and field – when a new year comes round.

Now I know everything:
how winter leaves without resenting spring,

lives in a safe time frame,
gives up so much but knows he can reclaim

all titles that are his,
fall out for months and still be what he is.

I settle for less than snow:
high only once, then no way up from low,

then to be swept from drives.
Ten words I throw into your changing lives

fly like ten snowballs hurled:
I hope to be, and will, long for this world.

You Won't Find a Bath in Leeds

From the River Cam and the A14
To the Aire and the tall M1,
We left the place where home had been,
Still wondering what we'd done,
And we went to Yorkshire, undeterred
By the hearts we'd left down south
And we couldn't believe the words we heard
From the lettings agent's mouth.

He showed us a flat near an abbatoir,
Then one where a man had died,
Then one with nowhere to park our car
Then one with no bath inside.
With the undertone of cheering
Of a person who impedes,
He looked straight at us, sneering,
'You won't find a bath in Leeds.'

'We have come to Leeds from Cambridge.
We have heard that Leeds is nice.
A bath is seen in Cambridge
As an integral device,
So don't tell me that a shower
Is sufficient to meet my needs,'
I said. I received a glower
And, 'You won't find a bath in Leeds.'

He fingered a fraying curtain
And I said, 'You can't be sure.
Some things in life are uncertain
And that's what hope is for.
One day I might meet Robert Redford
At Bristol Temple Meads.
I've found baths in Bracknell and Bedford
And I might find a bath in Leeds.'

He replied with a refutation
Which served to increase our pain
But we didn't head for the station
Or run for a rescue train,
Though we felt like trampled flowers
Who'd been set upon by weeds.
We told him to stuff his showers
And we would find a bath in Leeds.

Some people are snide and scathing
And they try to undermine
Your favourite form of bathing
Or the way you write a line.
At night, while you're busy praying
That your every plan succeeds,
There are killjoys somewhere saying,
'You won't find a bath in Leeds.'

A better definition
Might be reading all of Proust,
But the concept of ambition
Has been radically reduced.
While the London wits are burning
Their cash in the Groucho Club,
In Yorkshire we're simply yearning
To locate an enamel tub.

I win, Mr Bath Bad Tiding.
I have not one bath but two.
En-suite in the sweet West Riding
And no bloody thanks to you.
I may never run fast, or tower
Over Wimbledon's top seeds
Or hit sixes like David Gower
But I have found a bath in Leeds.

Out of This World

Cannot remember grass between my toes
or how it feels when feet and tarmac touch.
Cannot recall my life before I rose
and I have had to rise above so much

that first I hit the roof-rack of the car,
then my ascent bent back a lamp post's head.
I have, without exception and so far,
risen above a tower of what's been said,

above a mountain range of what's been done
to people, books and cities that I love.
I'll risk head-on collision with the sun
if I have one more thing to rise above.

What if the risen suffocate in space?
You send us up, not knowing where we'll go.
Would it be such a terrible disgrace
if just this once, I were to sink below

the quilted warmth of your intended slur,
your next offence, soft as a feather bed?
I'd prove more difficult to disinter
than knobbly tree roots or the tenured dead

and after having done my stint in blue
and subsequent to equal time in green
it will not matter if I dropped or flew
out of this world. Out of this world, I mean.

Wells-Next-the-Sea

I came this little seaside town
And went a pub they call The Crown
Where straight away I happened see
A man who seemed quite partial me.
I proved susceptible his charms
And fell right in his open arms.
From time time, every now and then,
I hope meet up with him again.

Six of One

I put it to my indecisive friend:
we step up our surveillance of the shops.
He shakes his head and says he'd like to spend
some time in jail, one year or two years, tops,
to ascertain which he prefers, the robbers or the cops.

He sighs and mentions double-sided coins.
He knows full well that his reaction peeves
his colleagues, but he argues if he joins
a bad crowd for a while, then when he leaves
he'll know for sure he likes policemen slightly more than thieves.

I say he couldn't stand two years inside.
True, he replies, *but think of my release.*
I can't confirm what's right until I've tried
what's wrong. He tells me I'm the one he'll fleece.
I grin. He might like confrontation rather more than peace.

Gently, I tell him not to be a fool.
Why not? he says. He tried the bottom set
before the top at comprehensive school.
I say *Remember....* No. He might forget.
He's not convinced that credit suits him any more than debt.

Listen, I shout, *that noise.* He bites his nails
while I pursue the yelp of an alarm
to a smashed window. As our siren wails
I grab my indecisive partner's arm
hoping by now he feels protection has the edge on harm.

He shrugs me off. No progress has been made
since his long, non-committal day began.
I scream *It's over! Finished!* – a tirade
that would provoke a more conclusive man.
He asks me why I think this sort of ending's better than

Seasonal Dilemma

Another Christmas compromise. Let's drink another toast.
Once more we failed to dodge the things that put us out the most.
To solve this timeless riddle I would crawl from coast to coast:
Which is worse at Christmas, to visit or to host?

To spend a week with relatives and listen to them boast,
Try not to look too outraged when they make you eat nut roast
Or have them drive their pram wheels over each new morning's
                                                            post?
Which is worse at Christmas, to visit or to host?

Dickens, you let me down. You should have made Scrooge ask the
                                                            ghost
Which is worse at Christmas, to visit or to host?

Second-hand Advice for a Friend

I used to do workshops in schools quite a lot
And some classes were good, although others were not,
And when sessions went wrong, in no matter what way,
There was one standard phrase every teacher would say.

Each time couplets were questioned by gum-chewing thugs
In reluctant time out from the dealing of drugs,
Some poor teacher would utter the desperate plea:
'Show Sophie Hannah how good you can be.'

This phenomenon cannot be simply explained
Since I don't think it's something they learned when they trained.
You do not have to say, for your PGCE,
'Show Sophie Hannah how good you can be.'

You do not have to say it to work or to live
But compared with advice that I've heard teachers give
Such as, 'Don't eat in classrooms' or 'Straighten your tie',
I've arrived at the view that it ranks pretty high.

Outside the school gates, in the world of grown men,
It's a phrase I'm inclined to recite now and then.
I don't see why I shouldn't extend its remit
On the offchance it might be a nationwide hit.

I've a friend who I reckon could use it. And how.
We've had a nice day so let's not spoil it now.
I am no kind of teacher, and yet I can see
That you're not in the place where you clearly should be.

No answering back – just return to the fold.
We'll have none of your cheek and you'll do as you're told
By the staff of Leeds Grammar, St Mark's and Garth Hill,
All those manifestations of teacherly will

Who join dozens of voices in dozens of schools
That make grownups of children and wise men of fools.
Stop behaving like someone who's out of his tree.
Show Sophie Hannah how good you can be.

Dark Mechanic Mills

A car is a machine. It's not organic.
It is a man-made thing that can be fixed,
Maybe by you, as you are a mechanic
Although I must admit that I have mixed
Feelings about your skills in this connection.
You shrug and say my engine sounds 'right rough'.
Shouldn't you, then, proceed with an inspection?
Looking like Magnus Mills is not enough.

Resemblance to a Booker Prize contender
Has a quaint charm but only goes so far.
When servicing formed the entire agenda,
When I had no real trouble with my car,
Our whole relationship was based upon it,
This likeness, but you can't go in a huff
If I suggest you open up the bonnet.
Looking like Magnus Mills is not enough.

I lay all my suggestions on the table:
Fuel pump or filter, alternator, clutch,
The coil or the accelerator cable
Or just plain yearning for the oily touch
Of a soft rag in a mechanic's fingers.
That's not your style at all. You merely grin.
Is it your Booker confidence that lingers?
I don't know why. You didn't even win.

You laugh as if you can't see what the fuss is
When I explain my car keeps cutting out.
I know that Magnus Mills has driven buses;
That's not the way I choose to get about.
I'm sorry that it has to end so badly
But I am up to here with being towed
And I'd take a clone of Jeffrey Archer, gladly,
If he could make my car move down the road.

Martins Heron Heart

No doctor cares enough
to analyse the content of my veins,
my blood that bears a rough
resemblance to a Stagecoach South West Trains
timetable. Start, please start,
Wokingham Bracknell Martins Heron heart.

Send a mechanic, quick,
the best you have. Should your mechanic fail
to get me going, stick
me on a train to Egham, Sunningdale,
Virginia Water, Staines.
It's true; those Waterloo to Reading trains

prove all your theories wrong –
medicine, science. I am on the mend,
doctor, thanks to a long
list of the Sunday running times. Attend
my bedside. Tick your chart.
Wokingham   Bracknell   Martins Heron   heart

Tide to Land

I know the rules and hear myself agree
Not to invest beyond this one night stand.
I know your pattern: in, out, like the sea.
The sharp north wind must blow away the sand.

Soon my supply will meet your last demand
And you will have no further use for me.
I will not swim against the tide to land.
I know the rules and hear myself agree.

I've kept a stash of hours, just two or three
To smuggle off your coast like contraband.
We will both manage (you more easily)
Not to invest beyond this one night stand.

To narrow-minded friends I will expand
On cheap not being the same as duty-free.
I'll say this was exactly what I planned.
I know your pattern: in, out, like the sea.

It's not as if we were designed to be
Strolling along the beach front, hand in hand.
Things change, of natural necessity.
The sharp north wind must blow away the sand

And every storm to rage, however grand,
Will end in pain and shipwreck and debris
And each time there's a voice I have to strand
On a bare rock, hardened against its plea.
I know the rules.

The Shadow Tree

In the lake, a reflected tree dangles
while its counterpart squats on the land.
Together they look, from some angles,
like a hand growing out of a hand.
Trunk to trunk, bark to water, they stand.

One is real, that would be the contention,
while the other, illusion or fake,
is a trick of the light, an invention
of the skin on the top of the lake.
I am here for the shadow tree's sake,

for its unannounced coming and going
(no one plants, no one chops). I would give
anything for a shadow tree, knowing,
as its branches get caught in the sieve
of the surface of water and live

for a glance of the moon, moments only,
that the dark fabrication I saw
was a miracle, not like the lonely
unexceptional lump on the shore,
such a stickler for natural law

with its sap, its botanical listing
and its representation at Kew,
its pedantic disciples, insisting
that one cannot be both false and true.
We are shadow trees. That's what we do.

He is Now a Country Member

He is now a country member.
The subscription rate goes down.
January to December,
If you live or work in town

You pay more. You come more often
And the fee, therefore, is high.
In a vain attempt to soften
Last year's blow, he now drops by.

Not a word since last September.
He left town. We both know why.
He says, 'I'm a country member.'
'I remember,' I reply.

Silk Librarian

We have a silk librarian,
One who behaves and looks
Just like a real librarian
When lending people books.
We lost our first librarian
Then others of her ilk.
We need a good librarian
And so we've gone for silk.

A silk librarian endures.
The paid and unpaid bills
Are neatly filed in metal drawers.
Eye-drops, inhalers, pills –
Gone. We no longer house the cures
For the imagined ills
Of real librarians with flaws
That far outweigh their skills.

Real flowers used to be displayed.
They died and made a mess.
Genuine salaries were paid.
Silk wages cost us less,
Though, over time, the colours fade
From eyes and hair and dress.
Every two years or so, upgrade
To maximise success.

Feel free to disapprove, protest
At what you never knew
Until just now, and never guessed
And cannot prove untrue.
A sin too many, once confessed,
Becomes a sin too few.
While you deny that silk is best
We cut the silk for you.

God's Eleventh Rule

I want to sit beside the pool all day,
Swim now and then, read *Peeping Tom*, a novel
By Howard Jacobson. You needn't pay
To hire a car to drive me to a hovel
Full of charred native art. Please can I stay
Behind? I will if necessary grovel.
I want to sit beside the pool all day,
Swim now and then, read *Peeping Tom*, a novel.

Pardon? You're worried I will find it boring?
My days will be repetitive and flat?
You think it would be oodles more alluring
To see the chair where Mao Tse Tung once sat.
Novels and pools are all I need for touring,
My *Peeping Tom*, *Nostromo* after that.
Pardon? You're worried I will find it boring.
My days will be repetitive and flat.

Okay, so you were right about *Nostromo*,
But I've a right to stay in this hotel.
Sienna: I refused to see *il duomo*.
(Does that mean Mussolini? Who can tell?)
In Spain I told them, 'Baño, bebo, como.'
I shunned the site where Moorish warriors fell.
Okay, so you were right about *Nostromo*
But I've a right to stay in this hotel.

I'm so alarmed, my voice becomes falsetto
When you prescribe a trip round local slums.
Would I drag you from Harvey Nicks to Netto?
No I would not. Down, down go both my thumbs.
I'm happy in this five-star rich man's ghetto
Where teeth are, by and large, attached to gums.
I'm so alarmed, my voice becomes falsetto
When you prescribe a trip round local slums.

It's not an English thing. No need to grapple
With the strange ways we foreigners behave.
My colleague would be thrilled to see your chapel,
Turrets and frescos and your deepest cave,
But as for me, I'd rather watch sun dapple
The contours of a chlorinated wave.
It's not an English thing. No need to grapple
With the strange ways we foreigners behave.

I want to spend all day beside the pool.
I wish that this were needless repetition,
But next to you, a steroid-guzzling mule,
A hunger strike and the first Christian mission
Look apathetic. God's eleventh rule:
Thou shalt get sore feet at an exhibition.
I want to spend all day beside the pool.
I wish that this were needless repetition.

Where to Look

The leaves that this year brought
next year won't bring again.
If autumn has one thought
it is not *where?* but *when?*

Summer is on the ground
long before winter's sting.
The loss must be profound
to make us hunt for spring.

Eyes down, we find it dead,
red powder at our feet
but staring straight ahead
we see its green wings beat,

all future and no past,
baffled as winter grieves.
Next year, not this or last,
is where to look for leaves.

Brief Encounter

I loved you and I left you at the station.
I watched you on the platform and I waved,
Taking in every scrap of information.
Every last detail of your face, I saved,

Thinking that when the engine started running
And as the train proceeded down the track,
You'd shrink, then disappear. But love is cunning:
The station café faded into black,

So did the world around you and beside you.
You alone seemed to grow. In broken hearts
Both distance and perspective are denied you.
Love looks no smaller as the train departs.

The Cycle

I cannot stay – I'm not the one deserting –
Or go; you are no longer here to leave.
I can't forgive, not without also hurting,
Forget, or I'll be even more naïve.
I can't confer; I'd feel that I was cheating.
I can't concede a case I've never fought
Or win and not administer a beating.
I cannot settle in or out of court,
Can't give in case I implicate the taker,
Can't take from everyone with ground to give
And gather acre on untended acre
When I need just a few square feet to live,
Can't end this in a neat or messy way.
I cannot start again. I cannot stay.

Black River

I asked to return to my original love
but I gave the wrong code and access was denied.
The clocks go back, though by no means far enough.
My white form came up green on the other side.
    It was so long since I had tried
that to do so was both a relief and a source of pride.

I asked to return to my original niche.
My house and furniture at Black River, I wrote,
then read it through. It read like a limp pastiche.
My white form came out smeared as a ransom note.
    I decided I must devote
more time to the box marked *Enter witty anecdote*.

I asked to return to my original ground.
Original, scoffed the clerk, *like there's such a thing.*
I thought his procedures all the more unsound
for being based on a rusty playground swing.
    Above us, a blackbird's wing
made a powerful case for never really bothering.

I asked to return to my original point,
but was that a person, a place or a state of mind?
A man in the queue shouted out *Let's split this joint*
so I shared my stash and he left it all behind
    singing *We, the undersigned,*
don't know. Then I wandered off, and what should I find?

Well, what I should find (though I cannot say that I did
since the arrows were keen to point towards something new
and all known rows, whether Savile, Death or Skid
had become the past, the ephemera and the view)
    is that none of it is true.
Go back to the starting line. Your original love is you.

The Cancellation

On the day of the cancellation
The librarian phoned at two.
My reading at Swillingcote Youth Club
Had regrettably fallen through.

The members of Swillingcote Youth Club
Had just done their GCSEs
And demanded a rave, not poems,
Before they began their degrees.

Since this happened at such short notice
They would still have to pay my fee.
I parked in the nearest lay-by
And let out a loud yippee.

The librarian put the phone down
And muttered, 'Oh, thank the Lord!'
She was fed up of chaperoning
While the touring poet toured.

The girl from the local bookshop
Who'd been told to provide a stall
But who knew that the youth club members
Would buy no books at all

Expressed with a wild gyration
Her joy at a late reprieve,
And Andy, the youth club leader,
And the youth arts worker, Steve,

Both cheered as one does when granted
The gift of eternal life.
Each felt like God's chosen person
As he skipped back home to his wife.

It occurred to me some time later
That such bliss, such immense content,
Needn't always be left to fortune,
Could in fact be a planned event.

What ballet or play or reading,
What movie creates a buzz
Or boosts the morale of the nation
As a cancellation does?

No play, is the simple answer.
No film that was ever shown.
I submit that the cancellation
Is an art form all of its own.

To give back to a frantic public
Some hours they were sure they'd lose
Might well be my new vocation.
I anticipate great reviews.

From now on, with verve and gusto
I'll agree to a month-long tour.
Call now if you'd like to book me
For three hundred pounds or more.

The Guest Speaker

I have to keep myself awake
While the guest speaker speaks.
For his and for procedure's sake
I have to keep myself awake.
However long his talk might take
(And, Christ, it feels like weeks)
I have to keep myself awake
While the guest speaker speaks.

Everyone in the Changing Room

Everyone in the changing room pronounced it a disgrace.
He'll get short shrift in Baildon if he dares to show his face.
He needs a damn good seeing to, that's what all his lot need,
      Everyone in the changing room agreed.

Everyone in the changing room reckons he's lying low.
The hot ones from the sauna want to tell him where to go.
The cold ones from the plunge pool say someone should start a
                                    fund.
      Everyone in the changing room is stunned.

Everyone in the changing room is certain it was him,
Young mothers from aerobics and the runners from the gym
And when they said it's mental, this, and there's no end in sight,
      Everyone in the changing room was right.

Everyone in the changing room would fight for this good cause.
We swim our lengths and lift our weights; you'll want us in your
                                      wars.
There will be no more tragedies, no waste or pain or loss
      When everyone in the changing room is boss.

Your Funeral

for L. W.

Since our routine condolences are sent
when someone dies, whether they're young or old,
even if while alive they were as cold
as they are dead, if sympathy's well meant,
why should ungrieving relatives resent
being unnecessarily condoled?

Why should the blood associates get cross
when bland acquaintances at wakes insist
how much the coffin contents will be missed,
how wonderful they were, what a great loss
it is? Form here is all. We can't just toss
bodies away (although we can get pissed

respectfully and in a mournful way).
People are hypocrites. Why should we care?
These days it's not expected that we'll wear
a scrap of black. We're not obliged to say
a single word. We can just look away.
Poor thing, the pain is more than she can bear

some well-intentioned neighbour dressed in black
will squawk, while we, in pinker shades of brown,
watch the undear departed get on down,
thinking of how we wouldn't have her back,
given a god-like choice, not for a stack
of cash, not for a kingdom and a crown.

Confident of the silence I'd maintain,
I was prepared. Then suddenly you die
and even silence seems too big a lie.
My strange regrets chase decades down the drain.
Can you still hear me now if I explain
how much I've always hated you and why?

Of course you can't. There's no such thing as you
or hell, with all its demons and its fears.
I should have told you in the living years,
as Mike and the Mechanics said. How true.
I didn't, though, and so you never knew.
Wreath after wreath arrives and it appears

You got away with it. My mother went
by plane to see you laid to rest abroad.
I told her yet again what I am bored
of telling her, that any money spent
on duty, guilt and other forms of bent
reasoning, one cannot, should not, afford.

She went. She said I didn't understand
and maybe if all mothers were as good
as mine, I would believe all daughters should
ʹbehave that well, cross air or sea or land,
even if they're afraid of flying, stand
beside their mothers in their crates of wood,

but when respects can't honestly be paid,
only ensure the death is genuine.
Reserve an empty pocket for a pin
(as did James Coburn in the film *Charade*).
Dig out a shallow oblong with a spade.
Insert deceased. See that deceased stays in.

Away-day

Dear baby the size of an olive,
Advise me on how to proceed.
On Thursday we've got an away-day
Which will be very boring indeed.

We'll be trapped in a room with no windows,
Doing things of no value at all
And I shudder to think how much nonsense
Will drift through the uterine wall.

You might hear the name David Blunkett.
Forget it as soon as you can
And look forward to treats that are pending
Like your first ever ultrasound scan.

Dear baby the size of an olive
I can't take you away from all this
But in seven months no one can touch us.
Think of all the grim meetings we'll miss:

All those votes for more rules and less freedom.
What a fine time I picked to conceive.
Down with what is now called education
And hurrah for maternity leave.

Mother-to-be

*Eating a good balanced diet, taking plenty of exercise and fresh air and finding the
time to relax when you're away from work will improve your chances of conceiving a
healthy baby... You should take particular care to cut down on 'social drugs'.
Cannabis is known to interfere with the normal production of sperm. It is also thought
that LSD can cause birth defects.*

(from *New Pregnancy and Birth Book* by Dr Miriam Stoppard)

Ideally your floors should not be carpeted but tiled.
A brightly coloured nursery will stimulate your child.
Do not eat soft-boiled eggs, smoke crack, fellate infected men
But tell your partner how you feel (see diagram, page ten).

You're bored and restless? Now is not the time to fly to China
Or to let friends with litter trays blow air up your vagina.
Make sure your fitness trainer is aware of your condition.
Remember, you must check your teeth and call that electrician

And every time you raise a glass or lift a fork, please think
Is this the very best thing for your child to eat or drink?
Once-a-month treats – a slice of cake – will not do any harm
But don't lick lambing ewes or stick syringes in your arm.

Quite often pregnancies go wrong, and when they do, that's sad.
It sometimes happens if you're stressed or pregnant by your dad
But eat your folic acid and next time a thin blue line
Appears, relax. Think positive. Most likely you'll be fine.

Try not to feel too daunted by this barrage of advice.
It really doesn't matter if you slip up once or twice –
Eat the wrong cheese, go on the game. It's not all doom and gloom:
Never again will baby be as safe as in your womb.

Now and Then

'Now that I'm fifty-seven,'
My mother used to say,
'Why should I waste a minute?
Why should I waste a day

Doing the things I ought to
Simply because I should?
Now that I'm fifty-seven
I'm done with that for good.'

But now and then I'd catch her
Trapped in some thankless chore
Just as she might have been at
Fifty-three or fifty-four

And I would want to say to her
(And have to bite my tongue)
That if you mean to learn a skill
It's well worth starting young

And so, to make sure I'm in time
For fifty, I've begun
To do exactly as I please
Now that I'm thirty-one.

Healing Powers

My foot is blue and bloated.
The swelling won't go down.
My limp is duly noted
As I hobble through the town.
I pass a Reiki master.
Of course! I should have put
The two together faster:
Healing powers, my foot.

I take my sore size seven
And place it in his hands.
It's ten now. By eleven
I'll be sprinting to the sands.
I ponder such remission.
My tears, like magic, dry.
Pure chance or superstition?
Healing powers, my eye.

My walking looks much better –
I jump, I jog, I hike,
Reluctant to upset a
Reiki master whom I like
But the pain is most dismaying
And I must confess, I put
New conviction in the saying:
Healing powers, my foot.

Homeopathy

She told me negativity was bad.
I said it wasn't, not the kind I had.

She told me that the people I resent
will have their own accounts of each event.

She said it wasn't up to me to judge
and that I should examine every grudge

and ask myself if those I cannot stand
are those who hold a mirror in each hand

reflecting back to me the awful fact
of who I am, unwelcome and exact.

She said there was no need to feel a threat.
I said suspicion was my safety net.

I'd allow harmless men misunderstood
if she'd allow the opposite of good.

Of course, she said, malevolence exists.
Respond with anger, though, and it persists

whereas apply benevolence like balm
and often you can soothe the rash of harm.

I did not feel my interests would be served
by spreading peace where it was not deserved.

What about standards, justice, right and wrong?
She said our meeting had gone on too long

and that the remedy that she'd prescribed
right from the start, if properly imbibed,

erodes those thoughts that play a harmful role
leaving what's beneficial to the whole

person (in this case, me). If this is true
then since I did just what she told me to —

taking my medicine, the right amount
at the right time — surely she can't discount

the feelings that remain. She should concede
that these must be exactly what I need

and that my grudge, impassive and immense,
is good for me, in a holistic sense.

I proved my point like a triumphant kid.
She laughed a lot. I gave her sixty quid.

Your Turn Next

You don't know where he's been.
You only saw him in a magazine,
                don't know what kind of life he's had,
        whether he's manic, violent, a fad.

        You don't know where he went
after the club, the sort of things he spent
                his pocket money on, the bit
        of trouble he was in. You don't know shit.

        He is a scrap of text
to you. He is the words *it's your turn next*,
                deal of the week, the longed-for link
        between you and the thoughts you failed to think.

        You don't know what he means –
philanthropy or company or genes.
                Can he play tennis? How's his serve?
        Are you what he will grow up to deserve?

        Seventeen years from now,
after too many lagers and a row,
                I'll turn up. Yes in your backyard.
        It's your turn next, so take it. Take it hard.

        You misconstrue his tone.
You cannot seem to reach him on the phone.
                He swore those plants were watercress.
        He is a stranger and you want him less,

        a psycho boy. A lout.
You don't remember, as you throw me out,
                that, give or take a wait and see,
        I'm only saying what you said to me.

To a Certain Person

If one day I should find myself in pain,
In a predicament or in distress,
There's something you can do for me: refrain
From digging out my number and address.

Don't send your sympathy or kind regards.
Don't send your cash (as if you ever would),
Nor are your presents, telegrams and cards
Evidence that you wish me all things good.

You will profess to want to help. Then do –
A burst of honesty might make me smile.
Tell me that you believe I'm overdue
This, if not even more severe a trial.

Indulge yourself: applaud, rejoice, enthuse
And maybe soon I'll have some more bad news.

Instead of telephoning every place
that is connected in your mind to me
and then concluding I am hard to trace
when Jill at my recruitment agency,
despite your cloth shoes and your honest face
and all the charm with which you plead your case,
explains the rule (quite proper, you agree)
of client confidentiality,

why not pursue some of those little scraps
of paper where my number's scrawled in pen?
They can't have travelled far, unless perhaps
you've been to the North Pole and back again.
Look in the pockets of your shirts, the gaps
between your piles of books, shake out the maps
stuffed in your glove compartment. Businessmen
ask for a card; you've taken nine or ten.

In many botched attempts to be discreet,
you hide my number where it can't be found
even by you, which strikes me more as sweet
than irritating. On the underground,
at King's Cross, Ealing Broadway, Warren Street,
commuters shake it daily from their feet.
The way you must have scattered it around
defeats your object. One day it is bound

to fall unbidden from a jacket sleeve
not at a moment you or I would choose.
Lies will be called for, harder to believe
when the same number tumbles from your shoes.
This doesn't worry you. You're so naïve,
but all I know is, each time you retrieve
the number you perpetually lose
it is a minor triumph, front page news.

You tell me I'm elusive, and your tone
Is that of hunter after catching prey,
sort of *Aha, I've got you on the phone,*
I've tracked you down, you'll never get away.
Thank you for the initiative you've shown.
Long may your absent-mindedness postpone
and your continued scattiness delay
the wind that carries novelties away.

Leave

Look at the street lights in the square
That should project an orange sky,
Then note the darkness everywhere.
They do not work, and nor do I.

This television, lost at sea,
Emits an endless, wordless roar.
It needs to be replaced. Like me,
It is not working any more.

The sunken car beside the road
Whose hazards blink that extra mile
Wants nothing more than to be towed.
It won't be working for a while.

Neither will I. You mustn't mind
Or take offence if I suggest
You learn the art of being kind
To everything that needs a rest.

Notice the fifteen forty-nine
Never quite makes it out of sight.
There is a problem with the line
So it returns. I also might.

Ante-Natal

My husband doesn't want to hold the plastic pelvis model.
He tells the other husbands that it's bound to be a doddle.
He thinks the role of classes is to teach, not mollycoddle.
       He'll go so far, but not an inch beyond.

My husband is afraid of meeting women called Magenta,
Of sharing wholesome snacks outside the Early Learning Centre,
Of any exercise that's an incontinence preventor.
       He's friendly but determined not to bond.

My husband listens to my fear, tells me to overcome it,
Changes the subject to the Davos Economic Summit,
Decides that if there's pain he'll simply ask the nurse to numb it.
       He says he doesn't think it sounds that bad.

My husband mocks the books with their advice about nutrition,
He shocks the other couples in the coffee intermission
By saying Ziggy Marley seems in pretty good condition
       Despite the smoking habits of his dad.

My husband doesn't care if I'm a leaner or a squatter,
Says pregnancy is no excuse for reading *Harry Potter*.
He isn't keen on Stephanie or Amos or Carlotta.
       Leave it to him; he named our latest car.

On Father's Day my husband gets a card he's not expecting.
I say it's from the baby, with a little redirecting.
He doesn't blame my hormones or insist that I'm projecting.
       He tells me he's the father of a star.

On Westminster Bridge

I don't believe the building of a bridge
Should be an image that belongs to peace.
Raised eyebrow or the river's hardened ridge,
It wouldn't want hostilities to cease.
Aloof, on tiptoes, it deserts each side
For the high ground and, though it has to touch
Land that real lives have made undignified,
I don't believe it likes that very much.
It knows that every time we try to cross
To a new place, old grudges bind our feet.
It holds out little hope and feels no loss,
Indifferent more than neutral, when we meet
Halfway to transfer ownership of blame,
Then both of us go back the way we came.

Ballade of the Rift

Two enemies at once I lost.
It was a heavy price to pay.
I thought that I could bear the cost
Of an impromptu mercy day.
Now I'm invited out to play
And find I feel distinctly miffed
With no fracas, no feud, no fray;
I yearn to instigate a rift.

Wildly and wantonly I tossed
My horde of grievances away.
Above my inner ice and frost
I forged the sun's most radiant ray,
Now, with its heaps of UVA,
Summer's a burden, not a gift.
I miss the grime, the grot, the grey.
I yearn to instigate a rift.

I rue the day I blithely glossed
Over my foes' misdeeds, while they
Try not to boss where once they bossed,
Promise to honour and obey.
To look for peers among one's prey
Requires too great a mental shift,
And as they wheedle, cringe and bray
I yearn to instigate a rift.

Preachers and shrinks and healers say
Forgiveness gives the heart a lift –
Good on them. Be that as it may
I yearn to instigate a rift.

Wedding Poem

for Rachel and Ian

Marriage's rather grand accommodation
Can make a budding love succeed or fail.
We stumble in and ask for information
Regarding all the properties for sale
And marriage is the price-on-application
Castle with grounds, moat, lake and nature trail.

Some kid themselves and think they can afford it
And when their love runs out it's repossessed
While others, who do better in love's audit
And whose allegiances deserve the best
Because they are the best, those ones can lord it
Over the squabbling and half-hearted rest.

Today the castle has its rightful buyer,
Its asking price, and it will not be trumped
Because the bidding can't go any higher;
This is a love that will not be gazumped
By any other applicant, hard-trier
Or any living heart that ever thumped.

Marriage is love's new house. Love has invested
Its savings wisely, bought the place outright.
It has had several flats, and it has rested
Its head in many a hotel and campsite.
This is the best of all the homes it's tested.
This is where it will sleep now, every night.

Royal Wedding Poem

This poem was commissioned by the Daily Mail, *to commemorate the marriage of Prince Edward and Sophie Rees-Jones. It was never printed.*

I have attended weddings in the past
Where I'm the only person in the room
To harbour an intransigent and vast
Landmass of spite towards the bride and groom.
I have attended weddings with my coat
Buttoned against the hot, ecstatic horde
Throughout the service, wearing a remote
Glaze to appear above it all and bored.

At last, a marriage I can celebrate:
No choruses of 'Oh, you have to come!',
No one I liked once but have grown to hate
But must make small-talk with to please my mum.
Weddings involving nobody one knows –
What a good plan. I'll vote for more of those.

GODISNOWHERE (Now Read Again)

Sign outside a Bradford church

1. Go, Di. Snow here.

    (as read by a woman called Diane who is contemplating booking a holiday somewhere hot)

2. Go dis now her E.

    (as read by a concerned father who is hoping to persuade his teenage daughter to stop taking drugs by appealing to her in a more contemporary dialect)

3. God is now? Here? Now? Read again.

    (as read by a philosopher who, on finding himself unable to settle the question of whether the concept of an almighty is a temporal or a spatial one, decides he needs to do more research)

4. God is nowhere. Now read again.

    (There is no supreme being. You might as well settle for a good book.)

Metaphysical Villanelle

'We may or may not cease to exist' – conclusion of a long, late-night discussion about religion on an Arvon course at Lumb Bank

We have argued for hours and this is the gist.
After much confrontation, at last we agree:
We may or may not cease to exist.

First you scoffed at my view, then in turn I dismissed
Your opinion, but now we've discovered the key.
We have argued for hours and this is the gist:

There is either a god or we're all slightly pissed.
Shall we compromise, since it's now twenty to three?
We may or may not cease to exist.

If I weren't so exhausted I might well insist
That I'm right as a right-thinking person can be
But we've argued for hours and this is the gist:

We can all go to bed without fearing we've missed
Some great spiritual truth. Melvyn's got it, you see –
We may or may not cease to exist.

There isn't a sub-text. There isn't a twist
And who cares? Who would like a Ryvita with Brie?
We have argued for hours and this is the gist:
We may or may not cease to exist.

Squirrel's the Word

They're rats with bushy tails, you claim.
They bite and spread disease.
Despite the reassuring name
Of squirrel, they are wild, not tame,
And they belong in trees.

But there's a squirrel that I know
Who calls each day at nine,
Catches the croissant that I throw
And chomps it on the patio.
I think of him as mine.

He is both patient and polite
While I prepare his meal.
Squirrel's the word and it's the right
Word in his case, in fact he's quite
The squirrelish ideal,

So deconstruct him all you please
To bushy tail and rat.
Squirrel is still the name for these
Creatures with squirrels' qualities
And he is just like that.

First of the Last Chances

I stand back as the Skipton train advances,
having to choose too fast

between the scorn and sympathetic glances
of my supporting cast

all of whom think boarding this train enhances
my odds. I wave it past.

If I don't take the first of the last chances
I will not fear the last.

A Woman's Life and Loves

The next eight poems have been set to music by the composer Gabriel Jackson, and form a song cycle that was originally conceived as a contemporary response to the Schumann song cycle *Frauenliebe und Leben*.

View

I am not lonely. I pretend
that I am here alone.
I do not see your shuttered face
or hear your monotone

but stare instead at roads and fields
and bridges and the sky
and feel the sun's rays on my face.
However hard you try

to substitute your view for mine,
I see the things I see
and am no longer here with you
though you are here with me.

Equals

Each of my false apologies
I retrospectively withdraw.
Yes, there have been discrepancies
Between my conduct and the law.

I have done worse, I have done less
Than promises would have me do,
And as I cheat, as I transgress
I do not give a thought to you.

I sensed that you deserved it then
But took the blame and looked contrite
Before I did the same again,
Thinking the wrong was mine by right

And I enjoyed the risks I took,
The tricks I played, the daily scam.
I have done nothing by the book.
When I professed to give a damn

My smiles, my tears, my words were fake.
Cut me in half; the core was bad
And when you made your big mistake
I can't deny that I was glad

To see, so newly justified
By your descent from fair and true,
The times I lied and lied and lied,
As if I knew. As if I knew.

Postcard

The chances are that by the time you get
This postcard, I'll be home. I will have phoned,
Arranged to meet you and we will have met.
(That day, the day with nothing ruined yet,
No hasty lust or lingering regret,
Decisions and admissions all postponed,
Will be the best we have.) I will have toned
Down what I feel to pleasantries and owned
Up to no thoughts of you beyond the set
Formula: I admire your work. I bet
You will have done the same.
                                        Grateful for this
Chance to stay friends and keep our present lives,
We will arrange another date and miss
Another chance before this card arrives.

Match

Love has not made us good.
We still do all the cynics said we would –
Struggle like heroes searching for a war,
Still want too much, and more.

Love has not made us nice.
Elders and betters with their best advice
Can't stir us from our loungers by the pool.
We dodge all work like school,

Leave urgent debts upaid,
Cancel the solemn promises we've made
If loyalties or circumstances change.
Our thoughts are no less strange,

But love has made us last.
We do together all that in the past
We did alone; err not as one but two
And this is how I knew.

Bridesmaid

A smile or kiss is all you have to spare;
Never a bed, a key, an inch of floor.
All that I am, all that I have, I share,
Yet I possess not half as much but more –
        Double, I swear,
        Though you remain unsure –
Twice what I owned or hoped to own before.

There is no metal weighing down your hand.
You are not subject to the whims of kings
And claim that you will never understand
The pleasure or the point of two gold rings.
        For you no grand
        Passion waits in the wings
Just your own space. A woman needs such things.

Not me, I say. Of all the things to need,
I choose another mind, another face,
Someone of whom, if I were ever freed
I would be tattered remnants or a trace.
        What awkward breed
        Would crave, would even chase
What age and death will bring in any case?

Test

Not easy to relate
This plastic stick, blue line,
To an October date,
A child who might be mine.
Is the blue weak or strong?
How loud the seconds tick
With all that could go wrong.
This blue line, plastic stick
The packet says to use
And then at once discard,
Forgetting that to lose
All that you have is hard
And for a month or so
This plastic stick, blue line
Is all I'll have to show
For what it claims is mine.

Charge

My skin grows taut. What once was soft turns hard
Like silk stretched thinly over sponge or shell.
I count as many bullies in the yard
As any school child desperate for the bell.

Watching my body sprout its suit of arms
Makes me aware of what I must protect,
My charge, who nature won't allow my charms
Alone to guard, much less my intellect.

I fear the notion that I need a shield
But if I run, I'll only rock the cage.
As enemies advance across the field
Cover is no safe substitute for rage.

I am the bearer of a small élite.
I wrap my arms around it in the night
But can't defend a king with my retreat
Whose country is the stomach for a fight.

Favourite

Anyone who prefers the light
Has not explored the dark.
All those who miss the owl in flight
Will lean towards the lark.
She must have heard that Noah halved
The pairs inside the ark
And on its wooden side was carved
The favourite child remark.

I read the message, heard the cheers
And saw the bright award.
I sensed that down the miles and years
A man was overboard,
A man who had been left to drown
And yet remained afloat.
I rinsed the shell dust from my crown.
He swam towards my boat.

The sea is full of souvenirs:
The splinters of the ark,
Bent bottletops and leaking beers,
Noah just one more shark.
I chose the course that I preferred
And will not disembark
I set my compass when I heard
The favourite child remark

So see me now as cabin-hand,
Captain or mutineer,
The scourge or saviour of the land.
I must be both to steer
Free of this sea where, full of ploys,
Old moons resent new suns.
All of my children, girls and boys,
Will be the favourite ones.